DEPRESSION THERAPY GROUPS FOR CLINICIANS

Marina Oppenheimer, LMHC

© 2021 Marina Oppenheimer, LMHC
All rights reserved
Published in the United States of America
First edition,
ISBN-13: **9798704757634**

TO ALL THOSE WHO SUFFER FROM

A

TERRIBLE ILLNESS CALLED DEPRESSION

SUMMARY

Depression Therapy Groups: How Effective are they?

Session 1

Session 2

Session 3

Session 4

Session 5

Session 6

Session 7

Session 8

GROUP RULES

INTRODUCTION

DEPRESSION THERAPY GROUPS

HOW EFFECTIVE ARE THEY?

Several studies have shown group psychotherapy to be more effective than individual psychotherapy in a variety of settings. The depression groups we are going to be dealing with in this book will be psychotherapy groups, not support groups as in the case of bereavement groups. The basic difference between a psychotherapy group and a support group is that while in the former members' interactions with others will be used as a basis for clinical interpretation and intervention; in the latter the goal is to provide members with assistance and information on the topic at hand. In order to be effective, groups have to be homogeneous; in other words, members have to be of approximately the same age and cultural background. In the case of depression groups, it is well known that different cultures have different ways of coping with loss; as a result, ensuing psychological interventions will have to take into consideration the patient's cultural origin.

I will borrow from Irving Yalom some of his definitions that describe masterly the goal of group therapy.

Universality
The fact that all members will be sharing their experience of sadness with others who are in the same situation will decrease members' sense of isolation as well as the feeling of being different.

Altruism
The group is a perfect place for members to help each other and this is a curative factor in itself. Helping others allows members to forget themselves for a moment and focus on someone else's distress.

Instillation of hope
Members who are more informed on the etiology of depression and its treatment will become role models for those who are struggling with the initial stages of their illness.

Imparting information
This characteristic is extremely important for depression groups since it provides members with much needed information on community resources, books, videos and other self-help material.

Cohesiveness
A cohesive group will provide its members with a much needed sense of belonging.

Existential factors
Members will learn that pain and suffering are a part of life that needs to be accepted and integrated into the fabric of our existence.

Catharsis
Catharsis is the emotional relief from a distressful situation. By exploring and verbalizing their sadness, members will feel relieved and less anguished.

Self-understanding
This factor will allow members to understand how their depression is the sum of all previous losses, but that with the right help they will be able to accept and overcome.

Note: Due to the complexity present in the process of overcoming depression, the group should not be composed by more than 8 members.

SESSION 1

INTRODUCTIONS AND GROUP RULES

The group leader introduces him/her. Members do the same and, as they do, they will be asked to write their first names on labels so that every member knows other members' names. The leader then proceeds to ask members what in their opinion is a depression group and what brought them to treatment. This is a way for the facilitator to become aware of each member's goal for the group. After all members have verbalized their understanding of depression groups, the facilitator provides his/her point of view.

Facilitator: *"A depression group is a safe place where people who have lost interest in life can express and explore their feelings. A group is also a place where we meet with other people who are going through the same experience, and where we learn about other ways of coping with the isolation and hopelessness generated by depression. It is a well-known fact that there is neither a unique way to be depressed nor a set time to heal. As a matter of fact, everybody will go through a depression in his/her own way, and will heal at his/her own pace."*

Following the description of a depression group, the facilitator explains to members what the group rules are as well as the importance of punctuality and attendance.

Group Rules: (At the end of the book.)

Once group rules have been explained and understood, the facilitator will verbalize again his/her goals for the group.

1. To understand the process of depression.

2. To increase participants' motivation to overcome depression.

----------0----------

Activity 1 is distributed and completed. Members are encouraged to share their answers with the group.

ACTIVITY 1

- What brought me to this group?

- Is this the first time I attend a group? If I have already attended other groups, how was that experience?

- What do I expect from this group?

- Do I believe that depression can be overcome?

- If not, why not?

- What can help me overcome my depression?

- Do I look forward to a better life for myself?

- What would be a perfect example of a better life?

- Do I know anybody who has a good life?

- Describe that person's life.

SESSION 2

DIAGNOSIS AND THE GENETIC ETIOLOGY OF DEPRESSION

The group leader will start the session by providing the following information.

1. THE DIAGNOSIS

According to the DSM-5 (Diagnostic and Statistical Manual of Mental Disorders) the following criteria need to be present in a diagnosis of depression. The individual must be experiencing five or more of these symptoms during the same 2-week period, and at least one of the symptoms should be either (1) depressed mood or (2) loss of interest or pleasure.

1. "Depressed mood most of the day, nearly every day.

2. Markedly diminished interest or pleasure in all, or almost all, activities most of the day, nearly every day.

3. Significant weight loss when not dieting or weight gain, or decrease or increase in appetite nearly every day.

4. A slowing down of thought and a reduction of physical movement (observable by others, not merely subjective feelings of restlessness or being slowed down).

5. Fatigue or loss of energy nearly every day.

6. Feelings of worthlessness or excessive or inappropriate guilt nearly every day.

7. Diminished ability to think or concentrate, or indecisiveness, nearly every day.

8. **Recurrent thoughts of death, recurrent suicidal ideation without a specific plan, or a suicide attempt, or a specific plan for committing suicide**.

To receive a diagnosis of depression, these symptoms must cause the individual clinically significant distress or impairment in social, occupational, or other important areas of functioning. The symptoms must also not be a result of substance abuse or another medical condition."

Furthermore, let's remember that there are several types of depression: **Major Depressive Disorder, Dysthymia, Bipolar Disorder, and Depressive Psychosis** are some of them. In this group we are going to be dealing mainly with Major Depressive Disorder, which is a combination of two factors: environmental stressors as well as a genetic predisposition.

When a major depression is very severe it can lead to suicide.

2. THE GENETIC ETIOLOGY OF DEPRESSION

As per the **Anxiety and Depression Association of America**, *depression is the leading cause of disability in the U.S. for ages 15 to 44.3. Major Depression disorder affects more than 16.1 million American adults, or about 6.7% of the U.S. population age 18 and older in a given year. While major depressive disorder can develop at any age, the median age at onset is 32.5 years old. Studies have shown that it is more prevalent in women than in men.*

Although the precise genetic make-up of depression is unknown, there are many theories that try to explain the role of the brain in the etiology of this disorder. Most probably however depression is a multifactorial syndrome where not only genetics but also environmental factors play a role.

Of all the types of depression, Major Depressive Disorder is the most common one. *According to the **Stanford School of Medicine**, this syndrome will affect 10 per cent of the USA population at any one time*. This is also the most prevalent type of depression in families with a history of despondency. *In a study published in the peer-reviewed **American Journal of Psychiatry**, researchers at the **Institute of Psychiatry at King's College, in London**, as well as scientists at other research centers in Europe and North America, stated that the chromosome 3p25-26 was located in 800 families with a history of depression*. The conclusion was that almost half of patients suffering from episodes of depression can link their episodes to a genetic factor. However, this does not mean that genetics alone will generate a depressive episode; what it means is that individuals with a genetic predisposition for depression will be less resilient when facing environmental stress. Researchers concluded that genetic factors will play a more significant role in the case of severe depression or in recurrent episodes of this illness.

According to the genetic theory of depression, heritability is an important factor to consider. Although a history of depression in our family is a not a sure predictor of us developing the disorder, it will probably make us more vulnerable to depression every time we are going through a difficult time. Genetic vulnerability will increase our risk of becoming severely depressed when the going gets rough. Several studies have also shown that *a person is more likely to complete suicide if a family member has taken his or her own life or has a history of psychiatric illness…* (**Healthy Place.**) However, I believe that the decision of killing oneself has more to do with a learned behavior than with genetics. Consequently, if one of our family members has ended his/her life during a depressive episode, and we think of doing the same, our decision has more to do with the way our relative has coped (or not coped) with suffering than with our genetic makeup.

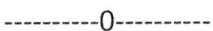

Activity 2 is distributed and completed. Members are encouraged to share their answers with the group.

ACTIVITY 2

The group leader will coach members on how to draw a genogram.

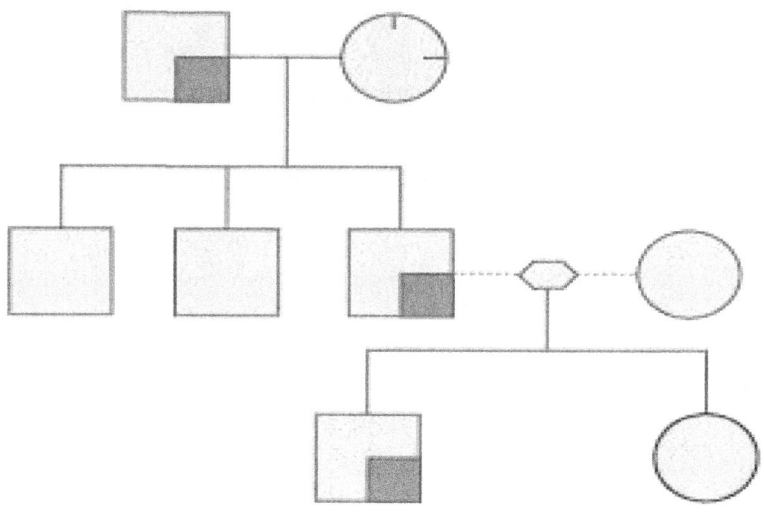

- M

(Get Word Templates; tree templates.)

- Use the lines below to show the relationship between your family members

    Normal: ------------------
    Distant/difficult: ------//------
    Enmeshed: =========
    Abusive: <<<<<<<<<<

- Show on your genogram which member of your family, if any, suffered from depression or any other mental illness.

- Do any of your behaviors when you are depressed remind you of any of your relatives?

- If you had a magic wand, what would you change in your family genogram?

- What would you not want to change in your family genogram? Why?

SESSION 3

ENVIRONMENTAL CAUSES OF DEPRESSION

"It's often said that depression results from a chemical imbalance, but that figure of speech doesn't capture how complex the disease is." (Fragment **Harvard Health Publishing**.) It is still not known what causes depression, but these mental states are probably not only the result of a chemical imbalance. The fact of being depressed is multifactorial, meaning that several factors play a role in generating a depression. Besides a genetic predisposition towards despondency, the following are some of these factors:

1. Loss
2. A difficult childhood.
3. Social isolation

1. LOSS

Undoubtedly loss is one of the major causes of depression. In this respect, it is important to understand that every loss we suffer in the present will rekindle all losses suffered in the past. This accumulative process is the cause of our sense of hopelessness and our feeling of being overwhelmed by our circumstances. However, we need to remember that not all people react in the same way to loss and environmental stress. Our personality will play an important role in generating or not generating a severe depression. Those of us who are not genetically wired to feel depressed will react to loss by grieving. Let's remember that while grieving is a normal reaction to life losses, depression is a clinical syndrome that needs treatment.

According to the **American Psychiatric Association,** there is a difference between the sadness generated by loss or bereavement and the feelings of depression. **While sadness can be intertwined with moments of serenity, a depression is an unbroken feeling of hopelessness**. Another important distinction between sadness and depression is the fact that while grief does not generate feelings of worthlessness, when we are depressed our self-esteem is significantly diminished. Since self-esteem is an important factor in regaining the interest in life, not having a healthy self-concept will no doubt interfere with our recovery.

2. A DIFFICULT CHILDHOOD

It is well-known that a difficult childhood plays a significant role in the etiology of depression. Growing up in an unstable emotional environment generates in the child a feeling of lack of safety. A child living in a physical or psychological abusive family will have more difficulties coping with life than children whose parents are emotional refuges. Physical or psychological abuse will erode children's self-esteem making them more vulnerable to psychological and physical illness. Between 1995 and 1997 the **ACE (Adverse Childhood Experience) study done by the Centers for Disease Control and Prevention and the Kaiser Permanente Health Plan** targeted almost 17,000 patients. The study's objective was to determine if there was a positive correlation between subjects' physical or mental illnesses and their adverse experiences in childhood. In fact, the study showed there was a link between the ACE score and physical and mental illness like depression and suicide.

I believe that when we are born into a dysfunctional family, we develop a pessimistic view of life and the world. Perhaps our parents suffered from depression or another mental disorder, or perhaps their parenting skills were lacking because they had not received from their parents adequate parenting. Since life is full of problems and difficulties, having a negative view of the future generates in us a feeling of hopelessness. In other words, when facing a difficult situation our life becomes a dark path to nowhere. Unfortunately, these dysfunctional parenting skills will repeat themselves through generations unless one generation decides to make a change and become healthier. If your parents and teachers were not emotionally healthy human beings, you still have the option to be the one member of your family who will change its idiosyncrasy for the better. Attending this therapy group offers you the opportunity to take a leap into the unknown and try other options. Let's remember that if a point of view or behaviors do not produce the results we are hoping for, we need to change either the point of view or the behavior. Starting to look at life from a more positive angle will help us build the necessary resilience to live a more meaningful existence.

If you happen to have children, overcoming your feelings of depression is extremely important. Let's remember that emotionally stable parents not only create for their children a harmonious environment, but also develop with them secure attachments. A secure attachment bond is created when the child feels that his/her caregiver meets his/her needs and protects him/her from the ills of the world. This security will have a significant influence in the child's development of a resilient and healthy personality. A child that feels his/her parent is depressed will resort to bad behavior because it is easier to tolerate an angry parent than a depressed parent. From the point of view of the child, an angry parent can take care of himself/herself, while a depressed parent is too vulnerable to take care of his/her child and of himself/herself.

Note: To find out your own **ACE score** or learn more about the ACE Questionnaire, please visit:
aceresponse.org

3. SOCIAL ISOLATION

According to psychologist **Erik Erikson's stages of psychosocial development,** the main goal of infancy is the development of a sense of trust in our caregiver. If we are unable to feel trust and on the contrary a feeling of mistrust develops, this will have dire consequences regarding our ability to establish with others close and intimate relations in adulthood. Another consequence of a conflictive relationship with our parents will be the fact that when looking for a partner, we will feel attracted by people who also have avoidant personalities; in other words, we will be looking for a familiar relationship pattern. The result of our difficulty to trust others will generate in our lives a feeling of deep isolation which will eventually end up in a depression. **Psychologist Terry Allen Kupers** stated that *"When I testify in court, I am often asked what the damage of long-term solitary confinement is... Many prisoners emerge from prison after years in solitary confinement with very serious psychiatric symptoms even though outwardly they may appear emotionally stable. The damage from isolation is dreadfully real."*

The best way to overcome social isolation is to reach out to others despite our fear of rejection. If we remember that the fact of being rejected has nothing to do with ourselves but with the person who is rejecting us, reaching out to others will be just another fact of life. Although rejection is a difficult pill to swallow, the best way to face it is to understand that in the same way that there are people we don't like, not everybody will like us. One thing to remember though is the fact that the relationships we establish need to be honest. Why do I mention honesty here? Because if our relationships with others are not genuine, they will not help us overcome our loneliness. In the more difficult moments of my life, I have always reached out to a friend to share my feelings. My goal was to learn how others had faced the same life challenges I was facing at that moment. Let's remember that we all see life and the world from different angles; a different viewpoint can open the doors to a path of healing.

In our current COVID health crisis, isolation and loneliness became for many of us almost unavoidable. Let's remember that not being in touch with others for a long time can result in a dangerous situation for vulnerable adults living alone. *"The results can be physical and emotional risks according to a new report from the* **AARP Foundation and the United Health Foundation.** *Two-thirds of adults say they are experiencing social isolation, and 66 percent say their anxiety levels have increased during the pandemic, according to survey results the foundations released in* **"The Pandemic Effect: A Social Isolation Report."** Because we humans are social beings, we need others to feel that our lives have specific goals and meaning. If we are unable to meet personally with others due to the risks of the pandemic, we should at least connect with them by telephone or other means.

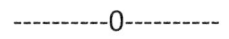

----------0----------

Activity 3 is distributed and completed. Members are encouraged to share their answers with the group.

ACTIVITY 3

- Would you say that when you were a child you were often sad?

- What made you feel sad?

- What would have helped you not feel sad?

- Did you have a mentor when you were young?

- If your mentor were here today, how would he/she suggest that you cope with your depression?

- Did you have childhood friends?

- Do you have good friends now?

- Are you able to self-disclose with a friend? Do you take into consideration his/her advice?

- What gives you hope in life?

- How do you see your life five years from now?

CHAPTER 4

THE TRAUMA OF LOSS

You will not overcome the loss of a loved one. You will learn to live without your loved one.
You will heal and you will rebuild yourself around the loss you suffered.
You will be whole again, but you will never be the same.
Nor should you be the same, nor would you want to be the same.
                    Elizabeth Kubler-Ross

Of all life stressors that we go through in life loss is the most difficult one to overcome. The path towards the reorganization of life after a significant loss is a long one. The more significant the loss, the longer and more difficult is the path towards having a normal life again. Our life is shattered, and we are pervaded by disorientation, sadness, apathy, loneliness and fear. Often the feeling of disorientation will lead to a lack of meaning and confusion regarding our beliefs. Our life as we knew it suddenly evaporates and all we see are debris all around us like after a deadly storm.

Deep down our hearts we all know that situations and feelings are not permanent. Throughout our lives we have all learned that **"this too shall pass**." However, human beings abhor change and we always have the tendency to go back to what is familiar. Unfortunately, life is nothing but change, and as Elizabeth Kubler-Ross states, losses are not to be forgotten but remembered. The only way to assimilate a loss is to find a meaning to what happened to us. However, this is easier said than done, especially in the case of the loss of a child. Moreover, what complicates matters further is the fact that since the meaning we are looking for is a meaning for us only, nobody can really help us in this complex task because nobody else has found the same meaning to loss. In his book **Man's Search for Meaning (1946) Victor Frankl** states that none of us can really avoid suffering; what we can do is find a meaning to what has happened to us. Finding a meaning to loss will provide us with a new purpose and will help us move ahead.

Furthermore, our life task is none other than that: finding a meaning to all that happens to us so that we can learn from experience and become wiser and stronger. Let's not forget that finding a meaning does not mean finding a way to justify the death of a loved one. It's just a way to understand how that loss is related to our life journey. Furthermore, even if we are unable to understand the loss, the important thing is our decision to go within looking for our inner wisdom. Although life journey can be a very painful one, I am convinced that it will never bring us more pain that we can bear because otherwise humanity would end.

When we suffer a significant loss, it is possible to enjoy life again, but the loss will stay with us forever. One of my patients who lost a daughter a long time ago told me recently that she still remembers her every day. However, another patient said to me that her daughter has been gone for so many years that she does not remember what her favorite dish was anymore. It is not uncommon for people who have suffered the loss of a loved one to see a vision of their beloved in their home for several months after the passing. This is none other than a symptom of their severe depression and their difficulty in letting go. All these symptoms have to be accepted as part of the grieving process. Gradually they will disappear as we move towards the reorganization of our life.

Kubler-Ross spoke of five stages of grief in the case of relatives of people with terminal illness:

- **Denial:** *"This can't be happening to me."*
- **Anger:** *"Why is this happening* to me?"

- **Bargaining** (before the loss happened): *"Please God make this not happen and I will…* (fill the blank.)
- **Depression:** *"I feel so sad that I don't have energy to do anything."*
- **Acceptance:** *"I am in pain, but I have finally accepted what is happening in my life."*

It is important to understand that we all grieve in different ways and that not all of us will go through Kubler-Ross' stages. Or perhaps some of us will go through some of the stages, but not all of them. It all depends on our life history and on the losses we have suffered in the past. Every loss in our life will rekindle our past losses so much so that we will not only grieve for our present loss, but also for all the losses that came before. In this respect it is important to mention that if during our first years of life our relationship with our caregivers was emotionally fragile, every loss that we will suffer later in life will be much more difficult to accept.

The process of grieving can be healthy or complicated. The symptoms of the latter are prolonged depression, i.e., lack of motivation to perform our daily tasks, anhedonia or inability to enjoy pleasurable activities, and often the wish to die to be reunited with our beloved. I remember one patient who was very attached to her father. The father suffered from heart problems and when he died and was being buried, my patient felt a strong desire to jump into the grave. Although she resisted the impulse, the intense feeling of loss stayed with her for many years until she was able to accept the death of her father as part of her life history.

However, loss is not all negative. As **Eckart Tolle** points out, loss and pain are our windows to a deeper reality where we will feel connected to all other human beings. Suffering is our road to becoming more compassionate beings. I once read that happy people don't have a history. It is true. It is only through pain that our life becomes wisdom.

"The natural way of being after the death of a loved one is suffering at first, and then there is a deepening. In that deepening, you go to a place where there is no death." (**E. Tolle, video on loss**.)

What Tolle means is that only the death of a loved one can give us the opportunity to reach that place where all is acceptance and peace. If we fall prey to depression, we will have a difficult time accepting reality and that peaceful place where all is acceptance will not be reached. On the contrary, when we are able to accept what is, we will reach that place in ourselves that goes beyond the reality we see towards a more transcendent place.

Life is a journey where challenges and hurdles need to be faced in order for us to go forward and become the human beings we need to become. Loss is one of those challenges and it presents us with the very difficult task of having to accept it and move on. Like those heroes who have to undertake a long journey and solve many riddles to become kings, we too have to learn how to face our losses one at a time.

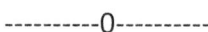

Activity 4 is distributed and completed. Members are encouraged to share their answers with the group.

ACTIVITY 4

From the below words pick one that best describes what you are feeling at this stage of your mourning process. Explain.

- SADNESS
- LONELINESS
- FEAR
- ANGER
- CONFUSION
- UNABLE TO EXPRESS MY FEELINGS
- FEELING DIFFERENT TO EVERYBODY ELSE
- UNABLE TO FIND A PLACE WHERE TO FEEL SAFE
- THE FEELING OF UNFINISHED BUSINESSES WITH THE DEPARTED
- THE FEELING THAT I WILL NEVER OVERCOME THE LOSS
- THE WISH TO DIE

Note to facilitator: If any of the group member's selects the last option, he/she should be directed to the nearest facility for treatment ASAP, or call 911 for immediate assistance.

SESSION 5

THE TREATMENT OF DEPRESSION

1. MEDICATION

Since depression is not an illness that is only generated by the body but also by life circumstances, treatment will usually consist of medication and psychotherapy. While the role of antidepressants is to balance chemicals in our brain so as to improve our moods, our sleep, our appetite, and our concentration, psychotherapy will deal with the cause of our depression and how to overcome it.

ANTIDEPRESSANTS

As per the Mayo Clinic *"Selective serotonin reuptake inhibitors (SSRIs) are the most commonly prescribed antidepressants. They can ease symptoms of moderate to severe depression, are relatively safe and typically cause fewer side effects than other types of antidepressants do."*

How SSRIs work

"SSRIs treat depression by increasing levels of serotonin in the brain. Serotonin is one of the chemical messengers (neurotransmitters) that carry signals between brain nerve cells (neurons).

SSRIs block the reabsorption (reuptake) of serotonin into neurons. This makes more serotonin available to improve transmission of messages between neurons. SSRIs are called selective because they mainly affect serotonin, not other neurotransmitters. SSRIs may also be used to treat conditions other than depression, such as anxiety disorders."

SSRIs approved to treat depression

"The Food and Drug Administration (FDA) has approved these SSRIs to treat depression:

- Citalopram (Celexa)
- Escitalopram (Lexapro)
- Fluoxetine (Prozac)
- Paroxetine (Paxil, Pexeva)
- Sertraline (Zoloft)"

How to follow an antidepressant protocol
By Greg Simon, MD; Kaiser Permanente

"Follow these steps when you start an antidepressant medicine. These steps will help you succeed with treatment.

1. Follow the self-care program.
2. Don't stop taking your medicine without talking to your doctor.
3. If you have side effects that bother you, call your doctor and ask for advice.
4. If you are not feeling better after 3 to 4 weeks, contact your doctor.
5. Don't stop taking your medication if you are feeling better. Ask your doctor first.
6. Take your medicine at the same time every day. Make it part of your daily routine. For example, take it at meals or when you brush your teeth.
7. Plan to check in with your doctor (in-person visit, phone visit...) after 1 to 2 weeks.
8. Schedule a follow-up appointment with your doctor about 4 weeks after starting the medicine.
9. If you stop taking your medicine too soon, you increase your risk for becoming depressed again (known as a relapse.) Also,

you might have side effects if you suddenly stop taking antidepressant medicine.
10. *Work closely with your doctor to make sure you have an antidepressant medicine that works well for you. Call your doctor any time you:*
a. *Have questions about your treatment, the medicine, or side effects.*
b. *Feel you are getting worse.*
c. *Think you can't stick with the treatment program.*
d. *You also need regular follow-ups with your doctor to talk about your medicine. Talk with your doctor about what kind of follow-ups is right for you (by phone, secure message, or in person).*

You should be in contact with your doctor:
1. *At least 2 times in the first month.*
2. *In about 4 weeks for a follow-up visit to make sure the medicine is working well for you.*
3. *Every few months after that.*
4. *For some people, tapering off medicine after 6 or 8 months is a good idea. People who have more severe or long-term depression should continue taking medicine for longer. Talk with your doctor about how long you should continue."*

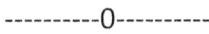

Activity 5 is distributed and completed. Members are encouraged to share their answers with the group.

ACTIVITY 5

This activity is designed to coach group members on the importance of following the antidepressant medical protocol as recommended. It is also important to encourage members to speak openly with their physician and request a different medication if the one prescribed is not working for them. Medications do not work in the same way in every organism.

- Have I taken antidepressant medication in the past?

- Did I follow the antidepressant protocol as recommended by the physician?

- Did I suffer any side-effects? Did I let my physician know?

- Did the antidepressant medication make me feel better?

- If it didn't, did I request a different antidepressant?

- Do I stop taking the antidepressant medication when I feel better without consulting with my physician?

SESSION 6

TREATMENT OF DEPRESSION

2. PSYCHOTHERAPY

COGNITIVE THERAPY FOR DEPRESSION

"Cognitive therapy was developed as a departure from traditional therapeutic approaches to mental illness.[5] While working with patients, Aaron Beck, a pioneer in cognitive therapy, observed that negative moods and behaviors were usually the result of distorted thoughts and beliefs, not of unconscious forces as proposed in Freudian theory."[5] (Stuart J. Rupke, MD; David Blecke, M.Div., M.S.W; & Marjorie Renfrow, Michigan State University College of Human Medicine, East Lansing, Michigan.)

"For many years it was thought that our brains stopped developing in young adulthood. Now we know that it is not so. Our brains and our personality can change constantly as a result of our life experiences. In other words, a new way of thinking can rewire our brain to think otherwise. **Neuroplasticity** *is the ability of the brain cells to adjust to whatever is going on in our lives and to create new synapses (connections) to different brain cells. Scientists sometimes refer to the process of neuroplasticity as "structural remodeling of the brain"* (Psychology Today.)

WHAT DOES NEUROPLASTICITY HAVE TO DO WITH DEPRESSION?

Being able to rewire our brain connections means that by changing our thoughts we can feel and behave differently. In other words, those thoughts that fuel our despondency by focusing on what we have lost can be replaced by thoughts that generate our capacity to enjoy what is given to us by life. By learning new ways of coping with adversity, we will discard our lifetime habit of resorting to thoughts of hopelessness. Our negative thoughts will be replaced by a more optimistic view of life and the world. This is how neuroplasticity and cognitive therapy play a role in teaching us how to transform our desperation into hope for the future; in other words, by modifying the way we think, our feelings and our behaviors will change. For those patients who do not respond well to medication (approx. one third of patients), cognitive therapy can be a wonderful resource that will help them overcome their despondency by thinking differently.

Greek philosopher Heraclitus (535 BC) once said that "**No man ever steps in the same river twice, for it's not the same river and he is not the same man.**" What this means is that there is no such thing as permanence; life changes continuously. It is the changes in our lives that generate loss, and it is our refusal to adapt to change that generates pain and suffering. If we could adjust to the fact that nothing exists forever and that this is a fact of life, time would help us overcome the pain of our losses and depression would not exist. Let's remember that depression is suffering that never ends. Coping with depression means to learn how not to allow our pain to control our life indefinitely.

On the other hand, change has also a positive side: if nothing lasts forever, then one day our pain will also diminish. **If we don't obsess over what is not with us any longer,** every new day will bring into our lives opportunities to start walking new paths. **Change is also the other term for hope in a different and better future**. If someone we love has left us, if we have been fired from a job, if a friend does not want to see us anymore, it means that those situations have reached the end of their road and that we need to start exploring new paths. In time new friends, new job opportunities, and even a new partner will become available as if generated by a magic wand (some of us call it Guardian Angel.) Change is also the opportunity to transform all those things that were not working in the past and to start over with different tools. Some years after my divorce, I was able to realize that the person I had married was not the person for me. Our separation gave me the opportunity to start a new and more satisfactory way of living. By accepting loss and change I was finally able to enjoy life again. When situations in our life end, accepting that finality is a fact of life allows us to generate new thoughts that have more to do with hope than with desperation. **For depression generated by the death of a loved one, please go back to the chapter on bereavement.**

CATASTROPHIC THINKING

Those of us who suffer from depression usually tend to be catastrophic thinkers. What do I mean by catastrophic thinking?

- Viewing our situation as a catastrophic event with no possibility of improving.

- Always focusing on the negative and discarding the positive elements in any situation.

- Looking at the future from the point of view of hopelessness.

- Being convinced that others are more able to cope with life than us.

- Being oversensitive and often feeling rejected by others.

In order to overcome and modify our catastrophic thinking tendencies we will need the help of a therapist. The clinician role will be to deconstruct our negative world view and replace it with a more effective and positive understanding of the events of our life. In this respect, whenever I am facing a difficult situation, my first thought is looking for a clinician friend to share my situation and request his/her feedback. Depending on our life histories, we all see the world from a different point of view. Listening to another person's reaction to an event is an excellent way of adding to our perception all those details that have eluded us. **Let's not forget that attention, like memory, is selective. We only see what we are used to watching.** A therapist can help us discover another way of looking at a difficult situation, usually with more flexibility and breadth of mind.

I believe that our feelings of isolation and hopelessness are our real hurdles to overcome depression. When we tend to see our future as a dark path that leads to nowhere, our vision has become too narrow; we only see what is not working. In other words, treatment will consist in creating a new reality, more flexible and more realistic. Let's remember that nothing is permanent on this earth; not even ourselves. **As a result, in order to live harmoniously we will need to be able to go with the flow of life and be confident that it will take us where we need to go.**

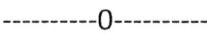

Activity 6 is distributed and completed. Members are encouraged to share their answers with the group.

ACTIVITY 6

In this activity the group leader will divide members in groups of two. In every mini-group one of the members will share with his/her partner a difficult life situation, and the other member will try to find a more positive way to look at it (it is usually easier to see the positive side of events in other people's lives.) At the end of the activity, every mini-group will share their task with the other group members. If needed, the group leader could extend this activity for more than one session.

SESSION 7

SUICIDE IS NOT THE ANSWER

I would like to share with my readers a personal story. When I was a teenager I was a very social person; probably because I was always looking for friends to compensate for the emotional distance I had to live at home. Not that my parents were indifferent; they were just distant like their parents had been with them. As a hypersensitive child, their emotional separation was difficult for me to cope with and I was always looking for affection elsewhere. When I was seventeen, during a summer vacation with my family, I fell in love with a handsome but not very good youth in my group. When after only two weeks he left me, I was devastated to say the least. One evening my parents decided to go to the movies while I stayed in the hotel room with a plan in my mind. As soon as they were gone, I gathered the aspirins I had bought that afternoon and lined them up on the bathroom cabinet. Then gradually, I began to swallow them one by one. But as soon as I had swallowed them all, I started panicking and went looking for my aunt who had not gone to the movies and was reading in her room. "*I took a lot of pills*", was the only words I was able to muster. She did not need more explanations in order to understand what I had done, and immediately sent someone looking for my parents. Fortunately, there was a doctor in the hotel who pumped my stomach and told my parents to stay away while he talked to me. He was a psychiatrist and I will never forget what he told me that night:

"Your best move today was to immediately regret what you did, so that we were able to save you. Be patient with life; what happens is what needs to happen for you to become wiser."

Undoubtedly, this doctor had read the Tao Te Ching.

Although I didn't feel well, the next morning I went to the beach and shared with my friends what I had done. Like only teenagers are able to do, they all listened to me with all their might; one by one they hugged me and told me how happy they were that I had not been successful. That day I felt happier than I had felt in months. I was learning to appreciate the beautiful things that were there for me, like for instance, my friends' affection. As the psychiatrist had told me: I was learning to focus on my blessings and letting go of what was not for me. If I mention this very personal event it is only because I want to show my readers that suicide is really not the answer. As soon as I had tried killing myself I regretted it, as I am sure many others did after taking such a tragic step. **I believe that a bout of depression is like having a fever: it shows up as an indication that some things in our life need to be cured and transformed.** Our best bet is to start analyzing what is not working and needs to be replaced with something more productive. In my case, what I needed to do was to stop looking for affection everywhere and select more carefully those destined to become my intimate companions.

The feeling of rejection that had induced me to take my life is a very dangerous feeling because we tend to think that we are the only ones being deserted while others have a wonderful life. Let me say that this is not so; regarding life struggles and pain we are all born equal. **When we reach out to others and they tell us how they also suffered feelings of depression and hopelessness at some time in their lives, we realize that we are not here to be happy but to be wise.** Understanding that life is difficult for everybody and that a perfect existence is a utopia will prevent us from comparing ourselves negatively to those around us. Buddhists recommend never wishing another person's karma; in fact, many times those whom we think have a better life have gone through more tragic times than us. **Besides, in order to regain our love for life we need to focus on our own life because it is the only life we really know.** Other people's lives are a mystery to us, and we can only speculate about its twists and turns. What we know about other peoples' lives is only what they want to show us, so let's not waste time in comparing ourselves to them. Instead, let's focus on what are those thoughts that pervade our heart with sadness, loneliness and depression; these are the thoughts that need to be examined and replaced with feelings of acceptance and hope in a better future.

----------0----------

The facilitator will distribute copies of Activity 7

ACTIVITY 7

- Think of a situation that was so painful and hopeless that made you think that suicide was an option.

- Since you are here today, it means that you overcame that situation. What were the thoughts and feelings that helped you reconsider the idea of suicide?

- What was the door that opened up suddenly in your mind that helped you move on?

- Was time a factor in your becoming more hopeful about the future?

- In your current situation, what are the thoughts that prevent you from seeing doors that are opening up in your life?

- Does the thought that life is not meant to be happy but to become wiser helps you change course?

- If so, what does the situation you are going through now can teach you? Please write a brief essay about this subject and read it to the group.

SESSION 8

WHAT IS DEPRESSION?

Although the etiology of depression is still unknown, we have already seen in previous chapters of this book that certain dire life situations can generate this disorder. Among them loss, loneliness, health problems, psychological trauma and stress are some of the events that can trigger a major depressive disorder, especially in those of us who have a genetic predisposition. **When we examine carefully these life events, we realize that their common denominator is the feeling of an injured self-esteem and of being disconnected from the rest of the world**. If we are affected by a severe illness, if we have been left or abused by a family member or a spouse, or if our manager at work is generating a lot of stress in our life, the feeling generated by these traumatic events is that of us being less valuable than others. When our self-esteem is injured by life events we tend to think that others are better equipped and more respected than we are. The feeling of being less important will not only generate in us a deep sadness but also the certainty that things will never improve. This state of mind is called depression. For instance, it is not uncommon that people going through a difficult divorce compare themselves to others whose marriages are still intact. This negative comparison will immediately trigger in their hearts a feeling of been less valuable than other human beings. At the same time, and even if they look for solace with some good friends, they will convince themselves that others are more skillful than they are at living the good life. Feeling less able than others of having a pleasurable life is the first step into the trap of depression. In the months and years that followed my divorce I used to walk my dog along the boardwalk; as I looked at passerby couples my usual feeling was that, for some reason, those women were more attractive and desirable than myself. After all, their partner was still there while mine had left me. Looking at things from that point of view made it impossible for me to climb out of the emotional abyss I had fallen into. It was only when I started focusing on my strengths and started using them to build a new life that I was finally able to return to my old non-injured self: the self I had before my difficult marriage.

Fortunately, there is a way out of a depression: it has to do with a healthy self-esteem. A couple of good friends are also necessary to overcome our feeling of hopelessness. When we feel extremely sad and alone it is very difficult to start following a more gratifying path. Furthermore, I know by experience that making good friends is very difficult; people are generally more concerned about their own issues than about helping others. However, there still are some good souls that have understood that we are all in the same boat and that someday they will be in the same dire situation as we are now. So, let's start by looking for some companions, one or two, with whom to share our moments of desperation. Once we find some people we can call when we need support, we start feeling protected and life seems less dangerous. Let me add here that, if we live alone, a pet is a golden asset in our battle against loneliness. Because it happened to me, I know that coming back to a solitary home is not the same as being welcomed by a jolly and festive creature who adores us.

The question however is how we can change our feeling of hopelessness and sadness into feelings of hope and psychological wellbeing. There is a medical term that will help us clarify this issue: placebo. What is the placebo effect? *"Let's analyze the effect from a medical point of view. The patient who received the placebo was totally convinced that his illness would be cured with this medication. This emotion is enough to start up the immunological system that will strengthen the resilience against the illness. In other words, since this positive thought has an influence from a psychological point of view, a placebo can obviously cure an illness.""* (The Art of Lying. Kazuo Sakai. Nakana Ide. Ediciones Paidós. 1999.)

What the author is telling us is that the power of our thoughts is undeniable: if we convince ourselves that we are valuable and that we deserve a better life, we will find the strength to overcome our lack of hope, and we will finally start our journey towards a more meaningful existence.

SO, HOW DO I CHANGE MY THOUGHTS?

STOPPING NEGATIVE THOUGHTS

Let's remember that the events we face in everyday life will generate automatic thoughts in our brain. Why is this important? Because our feelings are generated by our thoughts and if our thoughts are sad or negative, our feelings will be the very similar. It happens to me sometimes when I go for a walk to remember sad episodes of my life. Almost immediately my view of the world becomes somber and I lose all motivation to carry on with the tasks that await me. For some strange reason many of us tend to remember more the difficult moments of our lives than the happy ones; and if we don't react to this way of thinking we will fall prey of depression. **The brain is similar to any muscle of the body: the more you exercise a positive way of thinking, the more spontaneous it will become.** As we stated in the beginning of this book, neuroplasticity is the ability of the brain to establish new meaningful connections and to adapt to change. As a result, with some effort on our part we can change our way of thinking and create a more inclusive view of life and the world. **Saying STOP and banishing negative thinking is one**

way of modifying our thinking habits, and if we do it long enough, we will definitely change our brain's way of operating.

"Doing something over and over again doesn't just make it easier. It actually changes the brain. That may not come as a surprise. But exactly how that process happens has long been a mystery. Scientists have known that the brain continues to develop through our teenage years. But these experts used to think that those changes stopped once the brain matured."(Alison Pearce Stevens. 9/2/2014.)

Now that we know that the brain is on our side when we try to change our negative thoughts, let's find out what are other ways to rewire it. T**he first step is to stop our thoughts and reflect on what we were thinking when we suddenly became sad and unmotivated.** Or, if we are already suffering a depression, what are the most prevalent thoughts in our mind. Once we know what these are, we proceed to change them. Let's see in an example how this works.

Example
In old age it is very difficult to make friends. **My future years will be a time of loneliness and despair.**

It is true that as we age new friendships become scarce. However, there are steps we can take to start meeting new people.

- Register for a course at a local adult community center.
- Walk every morning to a park with a book, sit on a bench to read, and meet those who do the same. Or walk a pet and start a conversation with other pet owners.
- Register for a zoom class and suggest that after the course ends, the group meet at an outdoor coffee shop.
- Register for a Meet Up group with people our age.

- If we live in a condominium, we should find out if there are other people our age living alone. If so, we can write them a note with an invite to meet them.

I am not saying that taking these steps is an easy task. Unfortunately, when meeting others there is always the risk of been rejected. However, once we understand that being rejected has nothing to do with us but with those who reject us, we will be fine. **Finally, the most important step is to convince ourselves that, if we make what is necessary to overcome our feeling of hopelessness, life will give us a hand. Let's remember that life always gives us a hand if we do what life is requiring us to do.**

WHEN LIFE GIVES US A HAND

From my blog https://marinaoppenheimerbooksblog.blogspot.com

Although at the beginning of the pandemic spending a few hours at home had been a refreshing experience, after several months of being almost always alone in four walls I began to feel the need to be with others. Unfortunately, at my age large numbers of others were reluctant to leave their homes for fear of contagion. As a result, I began to feel that life had become a sequence of days without meaning. The idea of not being able to enjoy talks with my friends gradually became a thorn in my solitude. Then one day I reacted. I remembered that in almost every difficult circumstance I had to face I had always found a suitable solution; I said to myself that there was no reason for this time to be different. Since the virus was still alive and well, and solitude looked like a long road with no end in sight, I decided that my only option was to organize my days so as to have very little idle time. The morning hours were easy to distribute as I usually walk Max, the dog, and then I write until lunch. The puzzle turned out to be the afternoon when reading a book doesn't last more than two hours and the rest is free time. Since I only watch movies at night, TV was not an option. Although it's true that I live on the beach, for some reason that I have not yet been able to grasp I only enjoy it on Sundays. Perhaps the paternal mandates that stated that it's only appropriate to have fun over the weekend still resonate in my mind, or maybe I still haven't adjusted to being retired. But finally, one Tuesday afternoon, fed up with the political news and the threats of the coronavirus, I decided to go to the beach with a book. I opened the umbrella and, after placing the beach chair in the shade, I set out to enjoy the afternoon. Suddenly something caught my eye, and I saw a woman with dark glasses and a mask walk towards me as she greeted someone by waving her arms. I turned around to see to whom she was saying hello so effusively, but I saw no one. It was when I looked at her again that I realized that the woman was none other than my friend S. Needless to say, after years of not seeing her, running into her on the beach filled my heart with joy. I don't remember why we had stopped seeing each other; what I can say is that such an encounter convinced me once again that life always has an ace up its sleeve. After greeting each other, S sat under the umbrella and began telling me about her life in all those years in which we had been apart. Then it was my turn to talk about my life, and as I did, a warm feeling of joy gradually pervaded my soul. Hours went by quickly that afternoon on the beach; and as they did the feeling of emptiness that had tormented me earlier dissipated. After S left once again I thanked life for giving me a hand.

THE POWER OF MUSIC

Friedrich Nietzsche used to say that ***without music life would be a mistake.*** I have to admit that it took me a while to understand the real meaning of this quote. Until one day by pure chance I listened to the music of a Mexican composer, Ernesto Cortazar. Although I have always been a fan of classical music, especially Mozart, alone in my house during the COVID outbreak I wasn't longing to listen to Mozart. Perhaps the life stage I was going through needed something different, more in tune with whom I had been in the years of my early adulthood and who I was now. Being alone and divorced, with my son already having started his own journey, I needed to go back in time to revisit the beginning of my life; that time before the tests and trials. The first day I listened to Cortazar's music I felt like he had composed his music just for me: it spoke to me of the country I had left so many years ago, it reminded me of my youth, of my family of origin and of what my life had been before the sadness that came later. Listening to those notes transported me to that place in our heart where we are never alone because we are connected to our beginning. It was then that I understood what Nietzsche meant when he spoke about the music that makes us feel valuable, loved and deserving a meaningful life. You too reader can find the music that will distance you from the emptiness and the lack of hope. It will be like a window to the life that you deserve and that is waiting for you right there.

LEARNING TO APPRECIATE WHAT WE HAVE INSTEAD OF FOCUSING OF WHAT IS NO MORE.

It took me a long time to understand that what I lost or never had was not meant for me. Life only gives us what is supposed to be a part of our existence. When we lose a partner through divorce, we tend to think that we have lost something extremely precious. **However, if we review what our life with that partner was really about, we will understand that the divorce was the logic consequence of a mistaken decision.** Thinking this way will erase from our thoughts the desperation that follows this kind of loss. That partner was simply not destined to be our companion for life. Let's remember just the good moments and turn the page.

Instead let's give a good look to what is really there for us and learn to appreciate it. I have a friend who each time she takes a shower she thanks life for the pleasure of the warm water flowing over her body. Let's remember that many places in the world do not have the privilege of running water, warm or cold. By the same token, when I come home in the evening I feel blessed to have a place I can call my own: my blessed refuge in the world. On not so good days, I sit on the balcony and revisit all those thoughts that need to be reassessed and changed into more positive thinking. I am extremely lucky to be able to do this in my own home where no one will interrupt such private moments. Again, many people on this planet do not enjoy this luxury so I have to be grateful. Let's remember once again that life is not a journey of pleasure, and that the moments of joy are few and far between. That is why we need to be grateful for our blessings and use them to become wiser. I would like to finish this book by reminding my readers of Socrates dictum: **"The unexamined life is not worth living."** So, let's use our depression as our lantern towards a more meaningful life.

I wish you all an amazing journey of self-discovery!

ACTIVITY 8

This activity is meant to allow each participant to describe how the group was beneficial to him/her and what its most important component was. Each participant should start with the sentence:

What I am taking with me from this group is ... (expand.)

Participants can end their presentation by thanking other members for their help.

Alternatively, members can choose from the expressions in bold letters in the text and provide their own interpretation as to their meaning.

----------0----------

GROUP RULES

- Maintain confidentiality. Group members and leader will keep private everything discussed in group.

- Listen to others without interrupting. Wait for your turn to speak.

- Respect other group members even if you don't agree with their opinion.

- You won't be asked to participate if you don't feel comfortable. However, your participation is valuable for the group because we all learn from each other.

- Turn off cellular phones

- Comply with attendance. Every group member is an important part of the whole. When a member is not present the group will feel its absence.

NOTES

Printed in Great Britain
by Amazon